END
TIMES
CLARITY

A Quick Guide to
Understanding the End Times
Through A *Kingdom* Lens

EVAN DOUKAS

ISBN 978-1-964959-72-6

eBook 978-1-964959-73-3

CONTENTS

INTRODUCTION

I believe there has been much confusion throughout parts of modern Christianity regarding eschatology (the study of the End Times), in which we have potentially taken scripture *way* out of its historical context and original intention. I also believe that these confused perspectives have contributed to a culture of *fear* that is actually *hostile* to some of the most central teachings of Christ, His apostles, and the Gospel of the Kingdom, but more on that later! I hope you will join me for an introductory presentation to make an appeal to the world regarding these matters. Although this can easily be done in a very long, exhaustive, and detailed fashion, I am going to keep this as concise as possible for now.

Within a topic that has been a passionate "hot button" for many, I want to thank you in advance for an open mind, and most importantly, a heart of *unity*, as this was the heart of Jesus for us.

Differences in this area should never divide us, but instead we should always come together to challenge each other in honor, and grow up together into the fullness of Christ. As you are a capable and valuable child of God, hopefully led every day by the Spirit of truth, and a possessor of the incredible words found in the Bible, I fully respect your power to agree or disagree, and I encourage you to search this out for yourself.

One of the best sources we have for interpreting the Bible is the Bible itself. I believe we will see the End Times scriptures begin to flow *clearly* and *seamlessly*, once we understand the historical and cultural context as understood by the original hearers.

Now *that* is exciting.
Let's get started!

> *Inaccurate eschatology causes believers to:*
> *Wait for a king who already reigns*
> *Wait for a kingdom they're already in*
> *Wait to become what they already are*
> *Wait for power they already have*
> *Wait for an age that's already come*
> *Wait for victory that's already won*
> *Wait to do what they should already be doing*
> *- Anonymous*

PART 1:
THE COVENANTS

In order to *really* understand biblical prophecy and the End Times, it is extremely important that we understand the biblical covenants. In fact, just a basic understanding of these covenants and their *timeline* will greatly bless even our routine reading anywhere in the Bible, because it gives so much context and depth to the text. A covenant is an ancient version of a contractual agreement between two parties that is deeply heartfelt, and morally driven by promise and commitment. In this case, we will be discussing the covenants between God and His people, called Israel.

In the time of Jesus and the apostles (during the early first century AD), there are two main covenants at play. They are the Mosaic Covenant (simply referred to as the "Old Covenant") and the Messianic Covenant (also referred to as the "New Covenant"). These two covenants are so important to the culture of the Jewish writers that they also define two major ages of time. The time of the Old Covenant is also known as the Old Covenant *Age* (the age of the Law and the Prophets), and the New Covenant as the New Covenant Age (the age of the Messiah).[1]

Just like other biblical covenants, they were both ratified by blood through a sacrifice. In the Old Covenant, Moses (the mediator) takes the blood of bulls and puts half on an altar and throws the other half on the people, which was an indication of innocent sacrificial blood *covering* sins. In the New Covenant, Jesus (the mediator) takes His own blood (shed on the cross, which is placed on an eternal altar in the heavens) and gives it to the disciples and says, "take and *drink*," which indicated the forgiveness of sins — not just covering over them as in the Old Covenant, but actually cleansing the *inner* person of sin. The New Covenant is an inside-out, transformative covenant. It is why the writer of Hebrews describes it as an infinitely *better* covenant, because it doesn't merely cover over sin, but

---

1   There are other important covenants such as the Davidic Covenant (a covenant of kingship which Christ ultimately fulfills as the one who would sit on the throne of David, (and another known as the Abrahamic Covenant) a covenant made to Abraham in which His offspring, ultimately through His seed, Christ, would multiply, fill, and bless the whole world). These covenants run alongside the others, and live on forever in and through Christ. There is so much more that can be said about them, but for the sake of time, we will stay focused on the other two.

is powerful enough to cleanse the conscience and transform the inner man!

Each covenant also had terms. For instance, the Old Covenant had the Law of Moses (simply referred to as the Law), whereas the New Covenant has the Law of Christ, which is Love.

The sign of the Old Covenant was circumcision of the foreskin (outward), whereas the sign of the New Covenant was circumcision of the heart — an inward transformation by regeneration and a cutting away of the old nature.

In the New Covenant, animal sacrifice was replaced with Jesus, the spotless Lamb. Offering sacrifices to God is now understood as our lives lived: our bodies laid on the symbolic altar (as explained in Romans 12:1) and our gifts of heartfelt praise and thanksgiving offered up to God (Hebrews 13:15).

The Old Covenant temple was a physical place of connection with God, but now the *true* temple has become Christ and his followers as a living temple (Ephesians 2:19-22, 1 Peter 2:5, 1 Corinthians 6:19).

Instead of the genealogical priesthood of the Old Covenant, the New Covenant priesthood now becomes *all* people in Christ, described as the royal priesthood in 1 Peter 2:5 and 2:9.

We can see, therefore, what Paul meant when he called the Old Covenant a type and shadow of what was to come in the New Covenant. The old things were pointing to the *substance*, which is Christ (Colossians 2:17).

The Timeline of the Covenants

A common misconception is that the Old Covenant lives on with the New, or the Old just runs into the New, in a linear sort of meshing of Covenants. This is not true, and understanding their timelines is *really* important. The Old Covenant was a temporary, transient covenant that had an end. It was not meant to be permanent. It was meant to tutor people to Christ — to prepare for and point to the New.

In this theme, the writer of Hebrews concludes in chapter 8 (verses 6-13):

> But as it is, Christ has obtained a ministry that is as much more excellent than the old as the covenant he mediates is better, since it is enacted on better promises. For if that first covenant had been faultless, there would have been no occasion to look for a second.
>
> For he finds fault with them when he says:
>
> "Behold, the days are coming, declares the Lord, when I will establish a new covenant with the house of Israel and with the house of Judah, not like the covenant that I made with their fathers on the day when I took them by the hand to bring them out of the land of Egypt.
>
> For they did not continue in my covenant, and so I showed no concern for them, declares the Lord.
>
> For this is the covenant that I will make with the house of Israel after those days, declares the Lord:
>
> I will put my laws into their minds, and write them on their hearts, and I will be their God, and they shall be my people.

And they shall not teach, each one his neighbor and each one his brother, saying, "Know the Lord," for they shall all know me, from the least of them to the greatest.

For I will be merciful toward their iniquities, and I will remember their sins no more."

In speaking of a new covenant, he makes the first one obsolete. And what is becoming obsolete and growing old is ready to vanish away.

We will cover the "vanishing away" of the Old Covenant shortly, but what we see laid out here is the clear distinction between the two covenants: the inwardly transformative, regenerative nature of the New Covenant, and the important point that the Old Covenant would end, even "vanish away."

So, when did the Old Covenant end and the New Covenant begin? If a covenant is inaugurated with the shedding of blood, we know the New Covenant began at the cross when the pure and spotless Lamb of God was slain for the sins of the whole world.

Was it at the cross, when the New Covenant began, that the Old Covenant ended? Well, from a heavenly perspective, perhaps, but it did not necessarily end in its earthly practice yet, because those who rejected Jesus (along with his New Covenant) carried on with the Old Covenant system of worship and practices, ignoring God's faithfulness in sending their Messiah to them. The Old Covenant priesthood continued in animal sacrifices within its obsolete temple system. This was not only invalid, but a total dismissal of the cross by those who rejected him and had him crucified in the first place. The blood of Jesus was enough. Infinitely enough. So, the validity of the Old Covenant system, along with its animal sacrifices, ended in God's eyes, but this Old Covenant sacrificial system was still in place, operating for another 40 years after the crucifixion until AD 70 and the total destruction of the temple, Jerusalem, and its entire system of sacrifice and worship.

The Culmination of the Ages

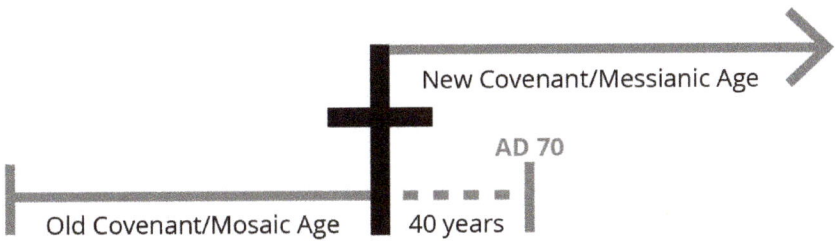

Before the event of its total destruction, the Old Covenant system severely persecuted the New Covenant believers (who became known as Christians). During this overlap of almost 40 years, it was a horribly difficult time to be a Christian. For those Jews who accepted Jesus as their messiah, it truly cost them everything, as well as their own families. This became equally true for the Gentile believers who had come into the faith by the wonderful revelation that, through Christ — Abraham's seed — salvation was for all people of all nations. Historically, it was at this point that Christians were heavily persecuted by both the religious establishment (the Jewish hierarchy, known as the Sanhedrin) and the political establishment (the Roman Empire).

This is why Jesus and the apostles continually encouraged God's people to endure, through hardships and even death, to the end of that generation (the 40-year period[2]) which marked the end of that age.

During the time of this persecution, it seemed as though nothing was changing in the religious order of things. The physical temple system with its animal sacrifices continued, right in the face of those who had put their faith in their Messiah. However, history tells us that tensions between Jerusalem and Rome escalated and came to its climax in the Jewish — Roman War and the Siege of Jerusalem. The cataclysmic fall of Jerusalem that followed, along with the destruction of the temple, marked a profoundly deep, consequential moment in history. It's truly *remarkable* that in so many Christian circles, these events are not taught, even in light of their deep prophetic implications and fulfillments. Understanding the events of AD 70 causes so many prophecies and themes in the Bible to fit together and make perfect sense for the reader.

In the next section, we will review a brief summary of what happened during this key moment in history.

---

2   It is biblically understood that a generation is approximately 40 years.

NOTES

NOTES

NOTES

_____

_____

_____

_____

_____

_____

_____

_____

_____

_____

NOTES

NOTES

PART 2:
AD 70

A revolt occurred in AD 66 amidst rising tensions between the Jews and their occupiers (Rome), marking the start of the Jewish-Roman War. From the beginning of the war in AD 66 to the destruction of Jerusalem and the temple in AD 70 was approximately 3 and a half years (or 42 months).

In AD 70, at the time of Passover, the Jews from all over the Roman world made their annual pilgrimage to Jerusalem, despite the tensions caused by the rumors of potential war. A siege began with the Roman legions surrounding the city. The

Jewish Zealots, who resisted the Romans at that time, torched and destroyed the city's food supply. This was an attempt to claim that God would intervene for their victory and to force their fellow defenders to fight the Romans. This move, as well as constant infighting between Zealot factions, caused mass starvation and the spread of disease. With resources depleted, death and unimaginable chaos ensued among the people as the surrounding Romans trapped everyone within the city walls.

Within five months, the Romans had successfully breached the city walls of the weakened resistance and soon after entered, massacring those remaining. The gruesome scenes described by witness and historian Flavius Josephus include very large heaps of corpses mounting up, blood pouring down the sanctuary steps, and cannibalism out of desperation. Escapers of the city were cut open because many had swallowed their gold in order to hide it from the Romans. (Many other such horrors can be referenced in Josephus' writings.)

Against the wishes of the Roman General Titus, some of his soldiers set the temple on fire, burning it completely to the ground. In the aftermath of this devastation, the soldiers dismantled every remaining stone in order to collect the gold that had melted into the spaces and cracks between them. Thus, the second temple (the center of the entire worship system of the Old Covenant Jews and all that was connected to it —the sacrifices, the priesthood, the idea of God tabernacling with them) was destroyed.

Massive numbers of Jews were killed during the brutal war, and most of the remaining were taken away into exile and slavery.

Even a general knowledge of these events is crucial to understanding the whole picture of the biblical covenants and prophecy. Scriptures begin to fit like a glove. In these next sections, we will see just how perfectly things come together in scripture, including the famous discourse found in Matthew 24 (the gateway to understanding the End Times) as well as the scriptures leading up to it.

NOTES

NOTES

NOTES

NOTES

NOTES

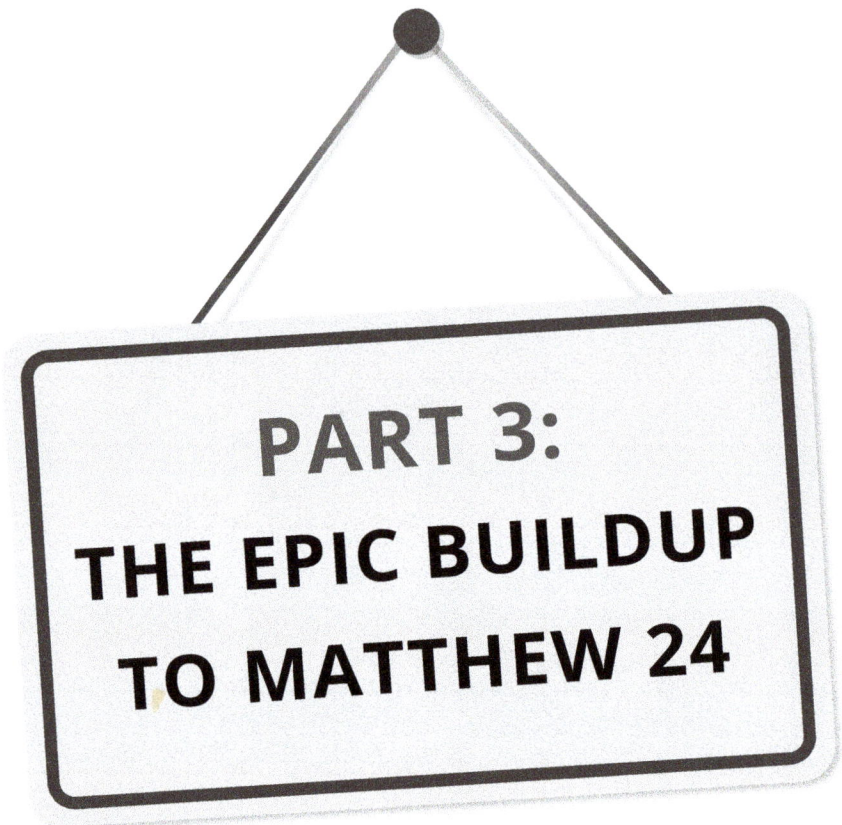

PART 3:
THE EPIC BUILDUP TO MATTHEW 24

The events of AD 70 were, in fact, forewarned for a long time. Throughout the Old Testament scriptures, we see God's warnings of the coming judgment to Israel for their unfaithfulness to the Old Covenant, as well as their mistreatment and killing of God's messengers, the prophets.

Judgment on a nation, throughout the Bible, was typically carried out in the form of being taken over or utterly destroyed by another nation, and Israel was no exception. The Bible records such events, and judgment of great magnitude was on its way when Jesus entered the scene. God's faithfulness to the salvation of his people, Israel, was found in their Messiah, whom he sent to them, but unfortunately, the Israelites who rejected his salvation would be subject to the wrath of the coming judgment.

As the herald of the Messiah forty years before 70 AD, John the Baptist boldly warned them to repent while announcing the coming of the Messiah — the one who would bring both salvation *and* judgment. In addressing the corrupt leaders, he states, "You brood of vipers, who warned you to flee from the coming wrath?" (Matthew 3:7) John knew that the imminent judgment was coming soon, and that many of those present to hear him were going to experience it in their lifetime if they did not repent! These were true warnings to the people standing right there with him.

Throughout the Gospels, we also observe Jesus calling the Israelites to repent from their destructive course, and warning of the coming judgment. Let's zoom in a bit as we build up towards Matthew 24 and stop in at Matthew 21 first.

In Matthew 21:33-46, Jesus tells the parable of the vineyard tenants, in which he paints the picture of Israel's past mistreatment of the prophets and predicts that they would murder him! (This is revealed with the tenants' stoning of the master's servants and the killing of his son.) Upon hearing the illustration, the chief priests and the Pharisees are asked, "When therefore the owner of the vineyard comes, what will he do to those tenants?" (vs. 40) Without yet realizing that Jesus was actually referring to them, they agree in their response that God will "put those wretches to a miserable death and let out the vineyard to other tenants who will give him the fruits in their seasons" (vs. 41). Jesus confirms their assertion and goes on to explain that the Kingdom will be taken from them and be given to a people who would produce its fruits.

Next up, in chapter 22, we see another parable with a similar warning and prediction. God (as the king in the parable) invited the Israelites to the wedding feast of his son. "But they paid no attention and went off, one to his farm, another to his business, while the rest seized his servants, treated them shamefully, and killed them. The king was angry, and *he sent his troops and destroyed those murderers and burned their city.*" (vs. 5-7) This is extremely telling of God's dealings with Israel through Christ. I recommend reading through it in its entirety, but again, this parable highlights Israel's rejection of their Messiah, their killing of the prophets, the subsequential opening of the Kingdom to the gentile nations (the people found on the main roads), and even the nature in which the judgment would come (the burning of the city in AD 70).

Then, in Matthew 23, we have Jesus confronting and calling out the leadership of Israel in an epic showdown. He ardently condemns their hypocrisy and follows with the "seven woes" directed right at them. In these woes, he accuses them of shutting the Kingdom of Heaven in peoples' faces, and calls them children of Gehenna, blind guides, greedy, self-indulgent, and white-washed tombs filled with dead people's bones, etc. Needless to say, it is not a good moment having the Son of God say such things about you!

Let's now zoom in to the last woe and the final statements found in verses 29 through 36:

> *"Woe to you, scribes and Pharisees, hypocrites! For you build the tombs of the prophets and decorate the monuments of the righteous, saying, 'If we had lived in the days of our fathers, we would not have taken part with them in shedding the blood of the prophets.' Thus you witness against yourselves that you are sons of those who murdered the prophets. Fill up, then, the measure of your fathers. You serpents, you brood of vipers, how are you to escape being sentenced to Gehenna [a place of fire and destruction]? Therefore I send you prophets and wise men and scribes, some of whom you will kill and crucify, and some you will flog in your synagogues and persecute from town to town, so that on you may come all the righteous blood shed on earth, from the blood of righteous Abel to the blood of Zechariah the son of Barachiah, whom you murdered between the sanctuary and the altar. Truly, I say to you, all these things will come upon this generation.*
>
> *"O Jerusalem, Jerusalem, the city that kills the prophets and stones those who are sent to it! How often would I have gathered your children together as a hen gathers her brood under her wings, and you were not willing! See, your house is left to you desolate. For I tell you, you will not see me again, until you say, 'Blessed is he who comes in the name of the Lord.'"[3]*

---

3   Interestingly, "Blessed is he who comes in the name of the Lord" refers to Psalm 118, which was historically read in procession during Passover. Remember that the siege of Jerusalem (the visiting upon Jerusalem by the Lord in judgment) took place during Passover!

A few things to note here: through these parables and passages, we now clearly have Christ's assertions of their killing of the prophets, the coming wrath of judgment, and *how* this judgment will come about, including fire, destruction, troops, the burning of their city, the desolation of their house (the temple), etc. Do these things sound familiar? How does it now fit in relation to the events of AD 70?

Perhaps most notably within this "woe," we not only see *how* but also *when* this judgment event would take place: "Truly, I say to you, all these things will come upon this generation." This fits perfectly within the timeline; *this* generation (the one he was in the midst of and addressing) would not all pass away before the judgment of AD 70, which would come upon them nearly 40 years later.

NOTES

NOTES

NOTES

NOTES

NOTES

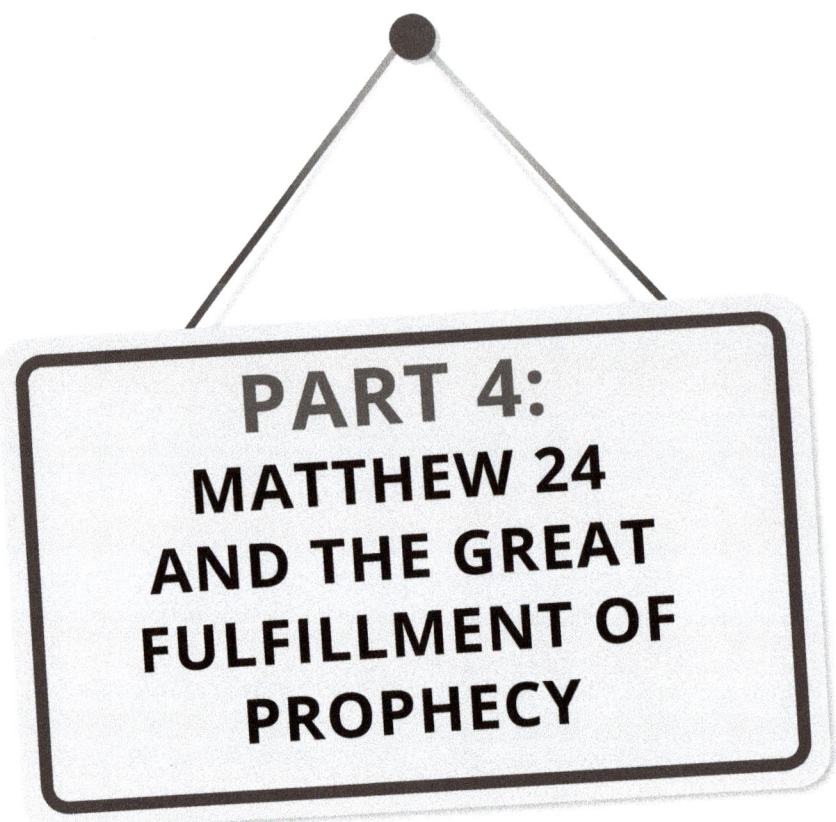

PART 4:
MATTHEW 24 AND THE GREAT FULFILLMENT OF PROPHECY

This brings us to the eschatologically infamous Matthew 24 discourse. It is also known as *The Olivet Discourse*, because the conversation between Jesus and his disciples took place while standing on the Mount of Olives, overlooking Jerusalem and the temple.

This is one of the most common and paramount scripture passages in End Times studies, and we will be looking at each verse of Matthew 24 in detail. Keeping in mind all that we have learned so far, let's begin.

Matthew 24:1-2

> *1 Jesus left the temple and was going away, when his disciples came to point out to him the buildings of the temple. 2 But he answered them, "You see all these, do you not? Truly, I say to you, there will not be left here one stone upon another that will not be thrown down."*

After the intense showdown in Matthew 23, including the seven woes against the scribes and Pharisees, Jesus again reaffirms the coming judgment upon Jerusalem, leading to its destruction.

Remember that in AD 70, after the Romans torched the temple, General Titus ordered his soldiers to take apart *every stone* of the temple to collect all of the gold that had melted in the cracks! This is clearly one of the greatest verifiable prophecies by Jesus. Yet, this prophecy is often misunderstood and misinterpreted because of a lack of knowledge of the events of AD 70.

Matthew 24:3

> *3 As he sat on the Mount of Olives, the disciples came to him privately, saying, "Tell us, when will these things be, and what will be the sign of your coming and of the end of the age?"*

The disciples' question provides the context for the rest of Matthew 24, and he is about to answer them thoroughly. Their question of "When will these things be?" implies that they understood the destruction of Jerusalem and the temple was on its way. In Hebraic thought, the *Coming of the Lord* (or *The*

Day of the Lord) was synonymous with God's judgment upon a nation. This is why they asked, "and what will be the sign of your coming?" (This will be further discussed and illustrated when we review verses 29 and 30.) The disciples are simply asking Jesus *when* this destruction and judgment will take place, and *how* they will know it is about to begin.

The third and final part of their question ("...and of the end of the age?") reasserts that the disciples knew they were part of the culmination of the ages, as covered earlier. They knew their Messiah had arrived, and so they were living to see the end of one age (the Old Covenant Mosaic Age, which they were in), and thereafter, the beginning of a new age (the Messianic or New Covenant Age to come). This judgment and destruction of the Old Covenant temple system would mark the final end to their present, Old Covenant Age. So, they were eager to know exactly *when* these things would occur.

Important note: In this verse, some translations erroneously read "the end of the *world*," which contributes to the misunderstanding of Matthew 24. The Greek word here is *aión*, which means "age," not "world."

Matthew 24:4-5

> 4 And Jesus answered them, "See that no one leads you astray. 5 For many will come in my name, saying, 'I am the Christ,' and they will lead many astray."

Notice in the following verses that the "you" Jesus is addressing refers to the disciples present with him, who asked him the questions in verse three. He is answering in a way that would be relevant to *them* and their peers. *They* would see these events unfold in *their* own lifetime (which we will see clearly as this discourse continues).

Historically, men coming on the scene claiming that they were the Christ actually happened during the time period to follow, and so it posed a threat to the first century Christians' faith and understanding of their true Messiah's words here. Two thousand years later, in the established Church, would it be much of a misleading deception if someone came on the scene saying that he is Jesus? Would Christians take it seriously, or would they more likely assume this person is a heretic or even mentally insane? But at the (First Century) time, as people all over Israel were speculating who and when the Christ would be, Jesus' warning to his followers was very relevant. He is warning them not to follow after others who would historically come claiming to be the Messiah, and so lead them into the coming destruction.

Matthew 24:6-8

> *6 And you will hear of wars and rumors of wars. See that you are not alarmed, for this must take place, but the end is not yet. 7 For nation will rise against nation, and kingdom against kingdom, and there will be famines and earthquakes in various places. 8 All these are but the beginning of the birth pains.*

Jesus' statement comes right at the time of the Pax Romana, which means "Roman Peace." While most of world history has been filled with war, the Pax Romana was a time of unprecedented peace in the Roman Empire (of which Israel was a part, as they were occupied by Rome), so this may have been quite surprising for the disciples to hear.

Yet again, in perfect prophetic accuracy, Jesus' words were soon to be proven true by rising tensions and conflict all around the region and within Jerusalem itself, increasing more and more as the culmination of AD 70 approached.

Historians, including Josephus, Tacitus and others, have written about these events, which marked the end of peace, as well as specific famines and earthquakes, regarding verse seven. Additionally, we can even find famine and earthquakes mentioned right in the New Testament itself (Matthew 27:51-54, Acts 11:27-29, Acts 16:26).

Matthew 24:9

> *9 Then they will deliver you up to tribulation and put you to death, and you will be hated by all nations for my name's sake.*

Remember who Jesus is addressing in this entire chapter: his disciples, the ones who would later be known as the apostles and would ultimately bring the gospel out into the world. Indeed, they would be persecuted and put to death, as history tells us. One does not have to look further than the book of Acts to see the accounts of this taking place in that first generation.

As mentioned previously, the first century Christians would also face persecution, not only from the Jewish religious establishment but the political establishment as well. Because of this, Christians faced massive persecution from their own countrymen in other regions and nations within the empire as the gospel spread and churches were established by the apostles. This worsened during the time leading up to AD

70 as Emperor Nero unleashed a great persecution on the Christians following the Great Fire of Rome in 64 AD[4], putting many to death.

It was a very difficult time to be alive as a Christian. It's no wonder that Jesus says, "they will deliver you up to tribulation" and John refers to himself as "your brother and fellow partaker in the tribulation" (in the present tense) to the recipients of his letter in Revelation 1:9.

All of the apostles suffered greatly for their faith and, in most cases, were brutally martyred for their uncompromising faith.

Matthew 24:10-13

10 And then many will fall away and betray one another and hate one another. 11 And many false prophets will arise and lead many astray. 12 And because lawlessness will be increased, the love of many will grow cold. 13 But the one who endures to the end will be saved.

The disciples and their first century companions would face many of the early Christians being led astray and falling away from the faith. The main issues they contended with were false teachers (known as the Circumcision Party and Judaizers) obligating the early churches to return to elements of the Law of Moses, as well as pervasive teachings such as Gnosticism and false prophecies. With heavy pressure of persecution in

---

4   The Great Fire of Rome was a catastrophic fire which caused massive widespread damage to the city, burning for 6 days in 64 AD. The ancient writer Tacticus reports that Nero used this fire as an opportunity to blame the Christians, and justify mass persecution of the Christians in the region.

the mix, it is no wonder that many Christians were threatened with falling away.

You can find these themes in many passages, including: Acts 20:29-30, Romans 16:17-18, Galatians 1:6, 2 Thessalonians 2:2, 2 Corinthians 11:3-4, 1 Timothy 1:18-19, 1 Timothy 4:1-3, 1 Timothy 6:20-21, 2 Timothy 1:15, Hebrews 10:25

This is why, throughout the New Testament, there is such a strong and urgent encouragement to endure and remain in "the faith."

Matthew 24:14

14 And this gospel of the kingdom will be proclaimed throughout the whole world as a testimony to all nations, and then the end will come.

There are multiple words that common Bible versions often translate as *world*: for instance, *kosmos*, meaning the world at large, all of creation, or the entire universe; and *ge*, which simply means earth as in land or ground. Another word . is *oikoumené*, which means the inhabited Roman world at the time.

For example, Luke 2:1 uses *oikoumené* when it states, "In those days a decree went out from Caesar Augustus that all the world [*oikoumené*] should be registered." Were they taking a population census of the entire planet, including South America? Australia? Of course not. This was relative to the regions and nations of the empire. (Note: One can easily search online for a map of the Roman Empire to view the expansive area it covered.)

Oikoumené is the word translated as *world* here in verse 14. This verse only makes sense when we realize the original Greek meaning of *oikoumené*; the Roman world.

Today, this verse is often taken way out of its historic context and originally intended meaning, where it is taught that the end will come when the gospel has reached every single country, city, town and people group on the planet. This is not what Jesus was communicating to his disciples, nor was he referring to the end of our planet. He was simply telling his disciples that the coming judgment (marking the end of that age) would not take place before they were able to reach the regions and nations under the Roman Empire with the gospel.

Was this fulfilled? Absolutely. The apostles successfully spread the gospel throughout the Roman Empire. The New Testament would later confirm this fulfillment:

> *First, I thank my God through Jesus Christ for all of you, because your faith is proclaimed in all the world. (Romans 1:8)*

> *[the gospel] which has come to you, as indeed in the whole world it is bearing fruit and increasing... (Colossians 1:6)*

> *He was manifested in the flesh, vindicated by the Spirit, seen by angels, proclaimed among the nations, believed on in the world, taken up in glory. (1 Timothy 3:16)*

Remember that this entire discourse refers to the disciples' questions about the event of his coming in judgment with the destruction of the temple at the end of the age! It is so important to keep historical context and reader relevance in mind.

Matthew 24:15-16

> 15 *"So when you see the abomination of desolation spoken of by the prophet Daniel, standing in the holy place (let the reader understand), 16 then let those who are in Judea flee to the mountains.*

There is much that could be said in breaking down the "abomination of desolation" (more properly known as "the abomination that *causes* desolation") which can be read about in Daniel 9[5], but to be clear and concise on this verse (15) which is often wildly misunderstood, one does not need to look any further than to observe the *parallel verse* of the same statement from Jesus in Luke's account, which reads: "But when you see *Jerusalem surrounded by armies*, you will know that her desolation is near. Then let those who are in Judea flee to the mountains." (Luke 21:20-21) It is clear that Jesus perfectly predicts the coming event of AD 70, even warning that the Roman armies would approach and surround the city, which is exactly what took place.

In verse 16, Jesus instructs the disciples (who would then also instruct all Christians who were present in the region) to flee to the mountains. This is a remarkable instruction by Jesus to save those who would heed his words. Walled cities were designed to protect those inside of them. While being

---

5   "And on the wing of the temple will come the abomination that causes desolation, until the decreed destruction is poured out upon him." Daniel 9:27b (BSB)

approached by the Roman legion, the intuitive response would have been to flee into the walled city of Jerusalem for safety. Instead, historical accounts confirm that the Christians did not do what everyone else did, but would get *out* of the city and flee to the mountains, where they would remain safe throughout the war.

If this verse is understood as something to take place in *our* future, 2,000+ years later, we would have to apply this to every Christian, worldwide. So, a modern Christian living in Denver, London, Sydney, or a small town in a far-off land, thousands of miles away from Israel, would need to flee to the mountains of Judea in order to be faithful to Christ's command. Again, we can see how historic context and reader relevance goes a long way in understanding the scripture!

Matthew 24:17-18

17 Let the one who is on the housetop not go down to take what is in his house, 18 and let the one who is in the field not turn back to take his cloak.

Similarly, we see that in warning his followers to be quick to escape the city, his instructions are perfectly accurate for those living in an ancient city whose houses had flat roofs that could be traveled across from one to another. They were not to lose time by going back down into their home due to the love of their earthly possessions. Or if they were already out in the fields, they were not to go back to their homes.

Matthew 24:19

> *19 And alas for women who are pregnant and for those who are nursing infants in those days!*

This is an especially unfortunate example of how a misunderstanding of scripture has provoked needless fear in many. It has been a heavy burden placed on women in recent generations. But once again, Jesus is referring to something that would happen in *their* near future — not ours. In this verse, various translations also use words like "dreadful," "terrible," and "miserable" in referring to how it would be for those women. Jesus was simply stating that this journey to safety in the mountains was going to be a hard one, especially for those who are pregnant and nursing (for obvious reasons).

Keep in mind that a letter of instruction in the Bible must be relevant to the recipients it was intended for!

Matthew 24:20

> *20 Pray that your flight may not be in winter or on a Sabbath.*

In a statement locked in a Jewish cultural context, Jesus was simply referring to the potential hardship of making the journey out of the region on the Sabbath when, according to Jewish law, one is only permitted a certain distance to walk. A "Sabbath Day's Journey" was limited to 2,000 cubits (3,049.5 feet, 0.596 miles, 960 meters). Of course, their journey of escape to the mountains would require many times greater distance than that, posing the threat of getting into trouble and being stopped by Jewish authorities while journeying out of the city.

Matthew 24:21

21 For then there will be great tribulation, such as has not been from the beginning of the world until now, no, and never will be.

In light of the events of AD 70 falling on the Jewish people, this was going to be tragic beyond comparison when we consider how truly deep the loss was. Not only were 1.1 million Jews killed in the most gruesome ways imaginable, but they also suffered the loss of:

- Their temple (It was the very place God dwelt among them.)

- Their priesthood (The records of lineage required for priesthood were lost with the temple.)

- The sacrifices (Without the temple and priesthood, they were no longer able to perform the sacrifices necessary to atone for sin and stay in a right-standing relationship with God.)

Essentially, their entire world and worship system as they knew it was destroyed.

It is also noteworthy, in this verse, that Jesus mentions this tribulation is "such as has not been from the beginning of the world until now, no, *and never will be*." The phrase "and never will be" indicates that there is still a future, and he is not referring to the end of the entire planet.

Matthew 24:22

22 And if those days had not been cut short, no human being would be saved. But for the sake of the elect those days will be cut short.

A more accurate translation of the phrase, *no human being* in the Greek reads, "not any" or "no one" would be saved, amounting to the potential of total annihilation of the Jewish people if the deadly siege had continued longer. At the end of the siege, as previously mentioned, a small percentage of Jews were taken to foreign lands as captives.

Also, it is worth noting that if the Roman war campaign had not ended when it did, they may have eventually discovered the Jewish followers of Christ hiding away in the nearby mountains.

Matthew 24:23-26

23 Then if anyone says to you, "Look, here is the Christ!" or "There he is!" do not believe it. 24 For false christs and false prophets will arise and perform great signs and wonders, so as to lead astray, if possible, even the elect. 25 See, I have told you beforehand. 26 So, if they say to you, "Look, he is in the wilderness," do not go out. If they say, "Look, he is in the inner rooms," do not believe it.

As mentioned in verse four, the first century was a vulnerable time for people to be misled by false messiahs, prophets and teachers, because the Jews (and therefore the early Jewish Christians) placed high importance on signs and wonders to support someone's words if such a person claimed to be from God.

Historians have recorded multiple instances of men coming on the scene claiming to be the messiah or a great prophet, leading the people out to witness their miraculous acts[6], or stirring them up in an uprising against Roman occupation. Many such instances were met with Roman force, including severe punishment or death. Therefore, Jesus is actually sparing his followers of not only the spiritual harm of following after another, but physical harm as well.

Matthew 24:27

> 27 For as the lightning comes from the east and shines as far as the west, so will be the coming of the Son of Man.

Building on the previous verse, Jesus reaffirms that the signs of his coming in judgment will not be something they need to search for in one place or another, and will not be a mystery revealed by a person who says they have the answer, but rather, it will be very obvious; as obvious as a lightning strike that can be seen from many miles away. The dramatic events leading up to the Roman siege and destruction of Jerusalem were anything but quiet or unnoticeable.

It is also worth mentioning that the historians Josephus and Tacitus consistently tell of celestial signs leading up to the events of AD 70, including an account of a sudden lightning flash that lit up the Temple.

---

6   In the Bible itself, we can see one small example of a false prophet performing signs and wonders when, in Samaria, a man named Simon stirs people up to follow him through performing acts of magic. Acts 8:9-24

Matthew 24:28

> *28 Wherever the corpse is, there the vultures will gather.*

The Greek word translated here as vultures is *aetos*, which is more commonly understood as "eagle" or "bird of prey." Translations like the King James, New King James, American Standard, Young's Literal and others read "eagles." It is widely known that the main symbol for the ancient Roman Empire, as well as the emblem on their soldiers' shields, was the eagle!

Once again, Jesus is eerily accurate in his prophecy, as the Romans (the *eagles*) would breach the city walls and enter into the horrific scene of countless *corpses* mounting up in Jerusalem.

Furthermore, this statement is also telling of the fact that so many would die, only to have their bodies be left to eagles, vultures and other animals of prey. This was a devastating reality in Jewish culture, which placed sacred importance on a proper and honorable burial of the dead. An honorable burial was evidence of a life well lived with importance and meaning.

Matthew 24:29

> *29 Immediately after the tribulation of those days the*
> *sun will be darkened, and the moon will not give its light,*
> *and the stars will fall from heaven, and the powers of the*
> *heavens will be shaken.*

Here is where things potentially get even further misunderstood, especially if we are unfamiliar with the historic and cultural context. The idea of these events having already taken place may sound like a shocker at first, but this *is* indeed the case, and it becomes clearly obvious once we turn to the Bible itself for interpretation.

Throughout the Bible, we see that the ancient Hebrews used a *lot* of dramatic, figurative imagery in their expressions, especially in their prophetic writings. Celestial bodies like the sun, moon and stars were understood culturally as symbols of governments, authorities, dominions and political states. Even early on in Genesis, there is a microcosm of this theme when Joseph (one of twelve brothers) has a dream about "the sun, the moon, and eleven stars" bowing down to him. His father, Jacob, responds with "What is this dream that you have dreamed? Shall I and your mother and your brothers indeed come to bow ourselves to the ground before you?" (Genesis 37:10) Without hesitation, Jacob knew that the celestial components of Joseph's dream had everything to do with the members of this chosen family. They each carried authority and dominion, whether patriarchal (Jacob —Israel), matriarchal (Rachel) or the brothers who, together, would embody the twelve tribes of Israel.

With this theme in mind, let's take a look at some events warned about in the Old Testament prophets, that we know have *already* taken place historically, and pay extra attention to the language used.

Isaiah 13 (NIV) refers to God's judgment on Babylon, during which the Medes would take over and Babylon would be destroyed. Referred to as "An Oracle Against Babylon," it reads:

9 See, the day of the Lord is coming

—a cruel day, with wrath and fierce anger—

to make the land desolate

and destroy the sinners within it.

10 The stars of heaven and their constellations

will not show their light.

The rising sun will be darkened

and the moon will not give its light.

11 I will punish the world for its evil,

the wicked for their sins.

I will put an end to the arrogance of the haughty

and will humble the pride of the ruthless.

12 I will make people scarcer than pure gold,

more rare than the gold of Ophir.

13 Therefore I will make the heavens tremble;

and the earth will shake from its place

at the wrath of the Lord Almighty,

in the day of his burning anger.

Here we have a prophetic warning to a nation about the coming judgment and destruction upon them, using the *same* kind of language that Jesus would hundreds of years later in Matthew 24! Isaiah did not mean *literally* that the celestial bodies would go dark, and that *literally* the whole world would be punished. He was using culturally rich, deep, dramatic, figurative imagery to express this coming judgment on a local region, as was typical of these ancient writers. The socio, political and religious governing systems of Babylon (represented by the sun, moon and stars) were about to be destroyed. The world as the Babylonians knew it was about to end, and this all came true historically.

Similarly, we have a prophetic word against Edom in Isaiah 34:4 (BSB)

> *All the stars of heaven will be dissolved. The skies will be rolled up like a scroll, and all their stars will fall like withered leaves from the vine, like foliage from the fig tree.*

And again, here is one against ancient Egypt in Ezekiel 32:7 (ESV)

> *When I blot you out, I will cover the heavens and make their stars dark; I will cover the sun with a cloud, and the moon shall not give its light.*

The events described in these passages were not literal (as we would not be here today if they had been), nor were they meant to be understood literally. Therefore, we can clearly see in Matthew 24 that Jesus was using familiar, biblical, prophetic imagery to declare the event of destruction on Israel, who had turned away from God and rejected their Messiah.

Matthew 24:30-31

> *30 Then will appear in heaven the sign of the Son of Man, and then all the tribes of the earth will mourn, and they will see the Son of Man coming on the clouds of heaven with power and great glory. 31 And he will send out his angels with a loud trumpet call, and they will gather his elect from the four winds, from one end of heaven to the other.*

This is another huge statement that often needs clarity. It may come as a surprise to our modern way of reading Bible prophecy (out of cultural context), but this illustration of God coming on the clouds is *also* figurative, prophetic imagery.

Like the previous statement from Jesus about celestial signs, we will review additional prophecies in the Bible where this language is found. But first, a word about the "tribes of the earth":

The word for "earth" in verse 30 is the Greek word *gé*, which simply means "land" or "region." Once again, this passage is a localized prophecy and is not referring to the end of the entire world. It is simply stating that the people of the remaining *tribes* of Israel inhabiting the *land* of Judea would mourn during this event.

In Isaiah 19 :1, there is a prophecy against Egypt that reads:

> *An oracle concerning Egypt. Behold, the LORD is riding on a swift cloud and comes to Egypt; and the idols of Egypt will tremble at his presence, and the heart of the Egyptians will melt within them.*

Did God *literally* come on the clouds to destroy them? Did the idols of Egypt literally tremble? Did their hearts literally melt? Of course not. God's judgment of destruction was historically fulfilled in another nation coming against them, and the same language Jesus used in Matthew 24 was used to prophesy this event. The disciples would have heard Jesus' words and known through their native language and culture that he was referring to his coming in judgment, the mourning of the Israelites, the destruction of Jerusalem, and the gathering of his believers to safety, which all were fulfilled in AD 70.

The following are a few other passages that show similar imagery found throughout the scriptures. Also, take note that the "coming of the Lord on the clouds" imagery is used to describe judgment *and* salvation.

"There is none like God, O Jeshurun, who rides through the heavens to your help, through the skies in his majesty." (Deuteronomy 33:26)

In reference to God coming to David's rescue and judging his enemies:

"He parted the heavens and came down with dark clouds beneath His feet." (Psalm 18:9 BSB)

"Behold, he advances like the clouds, his chariots like the whirlwind. His horses are swifter than eagles. Woe to us, for we are ruined!" (Jeremiah 4:13 BSB)

Zephaniah 1 refers to the historic Babylonian invasion of Judah and destruction of Jerusalem:

14 The great day of the LORD is near,
near and hastening fast;
the sound of the day of the LORD is bitter;
the mighty man cries aloud there.
15 A day of wrath is that day,
a day of distress and anguish,
a day of ruin and devastation,
a day of darkness and gloom,
a day of clouds and thick darkness,
16 a day of trumpet blast and battle cry
against the fortified cities
and against the lofty battlements.

Additionally, as it pertains to verses 27, 29 and 30 of Matthew 24, it is worth mentioning that the writers Josephus and Tacitus record actual signs in the sky, leading up to the Roman siege:

Besides these [signs], a few days after that feast, on the one-and-twentieth day of the month Artemisius, a certain prodigious and incredible phenomenon appeared; I suppose the account of it would seem to be a fable, were it not related by those that saw it, and were not the events that followed it of so considerable a nature as to deserve such signals; for, before sun-setting, chariots and troops of soldiers in their armor were seen running about among the clouds, and surrounding of cities. Moreover, at that feast which we call Pentecost, as the priests were going by night into the inner temple, as their custom was, to perform their sacred ministrations, they said that, in the first place, they felt a quaking, and heard a great noise, and after that they heard a sound as of a great multitude, saying, "Let us remove hence."

(Flavius Josephus, Jewish historian and witness, The Wars of the Jews)

In the sky appeared a vision of armies in conflict, of glittering armor. A sudden lightning flash from the clouds lit up the Temple. The doors of the holy place abruptly opened, a superhuman voice was heard to declare that the gods were leaving it, and in the same instant came the rushing tumult of their departure.

(Tacitus, Greek historian and politician, Histories)

Matthew 24:32-33

32 "From the fig tree learn its lesson: as soon as its branch becomes tender and puts out its leaves, you know that summer is near. 33 So also, when you see all these things, you know that he is near, at the very gates.

Jesus is obviously preparing his followers, making sure they are ready to escape the coming devastation by observing the signs (described in earlier verses) building up as the day approaches.

Matthew 24:34

34 Truly, I say to you, this generation will not pass away until all these things take place.

As we begin to understand End Times prophecies in their proper context, this verse finally makes perfect sense! Many of us have gone for years assuming that passages like Matthew 24 were about the end of the world and in our future, yet wondering why Jesus stated this in verse 34. In an attempt to make logical sense for a future point of view, I have heard it stated that Jesus was not speaking to the generation alive at the time when he said *"this* generation," but that he was actually somehow referring to a future generation that would be alive at the time of these events. In light of all that we have reviewed so far, let's consider how this might seriously neglect the context, and would render his words irrelevant to those he was speaking with at the time.

The futuristic interpretation also gets dismantled when we read parallel statements by Jesus in Matthew 16:28 and

Luke 9:27, which state that there are some standing there who would "not taste death" until these things take place at his coming.

In Luke 23:28, when Jesus was carrying his cross, there was a multitude of women mourning and lamenting for him. He turned to them and said, "Daughters of Jerusalem, do not weep for me, but weep for yourselves and for your children." This is an *exact* fit for the timeline we are discussing, as most of these women and their children would be alive less than 40 years later (in the devastating event of AD 70).

Furthermore, there are countless other statements throughout the New Testament about Christ's coming, described by the apostles using Greek words like *tachos* and *tachu* (meaning quickly, shortly, speedily), *eggizó* (meaning near, at hand, with extreme closeness, immediate imminence), and *melló* (meaning about to happen). Here are just a few examples out of many: James 5:8, Philippians 4:5, Hebrews 10:25, 1 Peter 4:7, Revelation 1:3, Revelation 22:10, 2 Timothy 4:1, 1 Peter 5:1, Revelation 1:19, Revelation 1:1, Revelation 22:6-7.

If these prophecies are yet to be fulfilled in our future, then Jesus and the apostles were wrong about their time frame — very wrong —by 2,000 years and counting.

But Jesus was *not* wrong, and neither were the apostles. The destruction of AD 70 happened to the generation Jesus was addressing in Matthew 24. It took place right at the end of the 40-year period from the time of his warnings, demonstrating the patience of God and his desire that as many as possible would repent, follow Jesus' words and be saved.

Matthew 24:35

> 35 Heaven and earth will pass away, but my words will not pass away.

Once again, a literal understanding does not do justice to the way the ancient audience would have understood Jesus, as they were well familiar with this cultural imagery.

As previously mentioned in Isaiah 34, which prophesied the destruction of Edom, we see the heavens being rolled up like a scroll and the mountains being melted with blood. The language involves destruction of "heaven and earth," yet it is clearly not literal and universal (since the event already happened historically, but we are still here!). It is figurative and local.

Furthermore, the phrase *heaven and earth* was a very common idiom representing God's covenant with his people, and the tabernacle (temple), which is the very representation of that covenant system.

As we find verses throughout the prophetic scriptures about either establishing the "heavens and earth" or the "heavens and earth passing away," we can see that he is referring to his covenant people and their temple either being established or destroyed, which took place multiple times within Israel's biblical history.

Regarding the devastating Babylonian captivity and destruction of the first temple, Isaiah encourages Jerusalem with a prophecy about their future restoration and reconstruction, using the idiom of a new heaven and a new earth.

Isaiah 65 states:

> 17 "For behold, I create new heavens and a new earth,
> and the former things shall not be remembered
> or come into mind.
> 18 But be glad and rejoice forever
> in that which I create;
> for behold, I create Jerusalem to be a joy,
> and her people to be a gladness.

And in chapter 51:

> 15 I am the LORD your God,
> who stirs up the sea so that its waves roar—
> the LORD of hosts is his name.
> 16 And I have put my words in your mouth
> and covered you in the shadow of my hand,
> establishing the heavens
> and laying the foundations of the earth,
> and saying to Zion, 'You are my people.'

Similarly, in describing the destruction of Jerusalem and captivity of Judah by the Babylonians, Jeremiah 4 states:

> 23 I looked on the earth, and behold, it was without form and void; and to the heavens, and they had no light.
> 24 I looked on the mountains, and behold, they were quaking, and all the hills moved to and fro.
> 25 I looked, and behold, there was no man, and all the birds of the air had fled.

26 I looked, and behold, the fruitful land was a desert, and all its cities were laid in ruins before the LORD, before his fierce anger.

27 For thus says the LORD, "The whole land shall be a desolation; yet I will not make a full end.

28 "For this the earth shall mourn, and the heavens above be dark; for I have spoken; I have purposed; I have not relented, nor will I turn back."

Can we see how richly metaphorical, figurative, dramatic and symbolic the ancient Hebrew writings are, and how important it is to understand this for interpreting the Bible? In our modern, literalist and linear way of thinking, it would be easy for us to dismiss their way of expression since it is quite foreign to us. (Many of our own ways of modern expression would be equally as puzzling to anyone unfamiliar with our culture!) But to do so would be a disrespect and dismissal of the very meaning and intent of the scriptures themselves.

Understanding the symbolism of the physical temple itself is also a vital piece to consider. It is important to realize that in Jewish culture, the temple represented (and was actually modeled after) heaven and earth. The outer courts represented the earth, the bronze laver (filled with water for ceremonial washing) represented the sea, and the holy places represented the heavens

We can see this described by the Jewish historian Josephus where he states:

"When Moses distinguished the tabernacle into three parts, and allowed two of them to the priests, as a place accessible and common, he denoted the land and the sea,

these being of general access to all; but he set apart the third division for God, because heaven is inaccessible to men."
(The Antiquities of the Jews, 3.181, Flavius Josephus, translated by William Whiston)

We can also find other writings that correlate the temple to "heaven and earth" in Psalm 78:69 and Jubilees 8:19.

The famous 1800s preacher Charles Spurgeon even recognized these themes quite well in one of his sermons, as follows:

Brethren, did any one of you ever weep because you did not sit at the Passover? Did you ever regret the Paschal lamb? Oh, never, because you have fed on Christ! Was there ever a man that knows his Lord that ever did lament that he had not the sign of the old Abrahamic covenant in his flesh? Nay, he gladly dispenses with the rites of the old covenant, since he has the fullness of their meaning in his Lord. The believer is circumcised in Christ, buried in Christ, risen in Christ, and in Christ exalted to the heavenly places. Did you ever regret the absence of the burnt-offering, or the red heifer, or any one of the sacrifices and rites of the Jews? Did you ever pine for the Feast of Tabernacles, or the dedication? No, because, though those were like the old heavens and earth to the Jewish believers, they have passed away, and we now live under new heavens and a new earth...The substance is come, and the shadow has gone; and we do not remember it.

As Spurgeon's statement reaffirms, the Old Covenant order (with its heaven-and-earth representation; the temple) was going to pass away, and Jesus' words (of his New Covenant order and Kingdom) would remain forever. (Hebrews 8:13 and 12:26-29)

Matthew 24:36-39

36 "But concerning that day and hour no one knows, not even the angels of heaven, nor the Son, but the Father only. 37 For as were the days of Noah, so will be the coming of the Son of Man. 38 For as in those days before the flood they were eating and drinking, marrying and giving in marriage, until the day when Noah entered the ark, 39 and they were unaware until the flood came and swept them all away, so will be the coming of the Son of Man.

This is often misunderstood and taken to an extreme as well. Just like the people in Noah's time did not expect the coming judgment of the flood, so also the unbelieving Jews would not expect the coming judgment of AD 70. Like Noah and his family, the Christ-followers were prepared for the events which their persecutors refused to see coming, and likewise, God would be faithful in bringing them safely through.

Matthew 24:40-42

40 Then two men will be in the field; one will be taken and one left. 41 Two women will be grinding at the mill; one will be taken and one left. 42 Therefore, stay awake, for you do not know on what day your Lord is coming.

This is not an illustration of the rapture (which is a newer doctrine that has been sensationalized in recent decades by thriller books and movies), but rather the opposite. In continuing with the theme of the story of Noah, where the wicked were washed away and the righteous remained, these statements highlight a biblical pattern of judgment. To be "taken" is often *not* a good thing. The righteous *remain* on (and inherit) the Earth. Psalm 37 also builds this case well, as it refers to the faithful ones *remaining* in and inheriting the land, and the wicked being cut off from it.

In John 17:15, Jesus prays for his followers, saying, *"I do not ask that you take them out of the world, but that you keep them from the evil one.",* but that you keep them from evil." We are not meant to be hiding out in escapism, waiting to be taken from the Earth to Heaven. We are meant to go out in Christ's authority, to boldly demonstrate the Kingdom of Heaven as his image bearers, and bring the realities of Heaven to Earth! Our awesome mandate is to manifest the prayer of "on Earth as it is in Heaven." The Earth is not a throwaway. God *loves* his creation, so much so that he gave his only son (John 3:16). We are called to *change* the world, not escape from it.

Matthew 24:43-51

43 But know this, that if the master of the house had known in what part of the night the thief was coming, he would have stayed awake and would not have let his house be broken into. 44 Therefore you also must be ready, for the Son of Man is coming at an hour you do not expect. 45 Who then is the faithful and wise servant, whom his master has set over his household, to give them their food at the proper time? 46 Blessed is that servant whom his master will find so doing when he comes. 47 Truly, I say to you, he will set him over all his possessions. 48 But if that wicked servant says to himself, "My master is delayed," 49 and begins to beat his fellow servants and eats and drinks with drunkards, 50 the master of that servant will come on a day when he does not expect him and at an hour he does not know 51 and will cut him in pieces and put him with the hypocrites. In that place there will be weeping and gnashing of teeth.

Having answered his disciples' questions thoroughly, Jesus concludes with a set of intense statements that underscore the importance of being faithful and prepared for his coming in judgment, as destruction will overtake those who do not follow him (or his words) in an unforeseen fashion. His illustrations highlight the severe consequences for those who are unfaithful and unprepared, because they would suffer the coming fires of destruction for rejecting his warnings. Those who rejected their messiah would soon find themselves on the outside of covenantal relationship and blessing. Having enjoyed the privileges of the Old Covenant, which was soon to pass away, they would now be in the spiritual domain of "outer darkness."

NOTES

NOTES

NOTES

NOTES

SO, NOW WHAT?

FINAL THOUGHTS

After reading this study, I hope you have some strong takeaways or new considerations which ultimately amount to freedom and fruitfulness in your life. Many questions may have surfaced (as this was more of an introduction to understanding End Times prophecy and certainly not an exhaustive and complete work), and such questions are an amazing doorway to the greater understanding we seek. Because of a lack of knowledge of historical events, the modern church has often over-complicated and sensationalized eschatology, creating massive fear and hysteria. Therefore, I wanted to propose an entirely different grid of understanding, one that removes fear and points us to the Kingdom of God.

I believe that eschatology must ultimately align with the victorious expansion of the Kingdom of God, a theme that is found all throughout scripture. For instance, Ephesians 1:20-23 reads:

> *...he raised him [Christ] from the dead and seated him at his right hand in the heavenly places, far above all rule and authority and power and dominion, and above every name that is named, not only in this age but also in the one to come. And he put all things under his feet and gave him as head over all things to the church, which is his body, the fullness of him who fills all in all.*

The Young's Literal Translation of verse 22 reads, "the fullness of Him who is *filling* the all in all," present tense. The Kingdom expansion (or *filling*) is not in one quick moment, but a glorious *process* of the restoration and saturation of all things. This process involves you. We, as His body, filling the "all in all," are the means to this end! Isaiah mentions this idea when he writes: "Of the *increase* of his government and of peace there will be no end!" (verse 9:3) What started small, as a single seed, was designed to increase, and is forever growing.

Recall the parable of the mustard seed that becomes the largest tree in the garden, and the parable of the leaven that works through the whole loaf. In Daniel 2, it is the mountain that grows to cover the whole Earth. It is not about changing everything instantly. It is about saturating all things with the culture of heaven — the goodness and love of Christ — until all of the Earth is completely filled in a beautiful process called the Restoration of All Things. As Numbers 14:21 states, "But as truly as I live, all the earth shall be filled with the glory of the Lord." (KJV)

This gradual growth of the Kingdom (the King's domain) is the purpose for why we are here. As the sons of God, we are to manifest Christ (no matter how bad things may seem), which is what all creation is eagerly waiting for (Romans 8). We, as God's people, are the light of the world (Matthew 5:14). We are his "A-team." We are not a Plan B (as some modern teachings suggest), a side thought, or a damsel in distress, waiting to be rescued. We *have been* rescued, and we are bringing the realities of that rescue and restoration to the world around us. Heaven invades Earth just a little bit more each time you and I bring forth on Earth what is in heaven.

Contrary to what is often preached, I believe we need to begin building, creating and inventing things again, establishing his Kingdom with the long view in mind again! Are we just quickly preaching a drive-by gospel (simply just getting someone to say a prayer), or are we actually making disciples and building relationships? Are we establishing his Kingdom culture for the long haul and sowing into the next generations? Or are we neglecting these things because we are yet another generation that erroneously thinks we're the last one? It is tragic when we don't invest in the future because we don't think there is one! It is sad to see the Church spend so much time and resources falsely predicting "the end of the world" (time and time again), instead of forging the future. What we believe about the future has a great impact on how we live today. When we realize the apocalyptic events laid out by Jesus are actually in the past, and that the Kingdom of God is in our midst, we are free to live it and build it, instead of waiting for something that is already here.

Jesus said that the Kingdom was "at hand" 2,000 years ago. That means, for us, the Kingdom is already here, *now* (Matthew 12:28). Jesus is ruling on the throne, above all, until all of his enemies are made a footstool under his feet. Oh, that we would *see* that the Kingdom already came and is here, *now!* It is not a physical thing to make a sudden, physical appearance so that we can say, "Here it is," or "It's over there." Rather, it is *within* every believer (Luke 17:21). Jesus so desires that we go forth with his authority to change the world — not hide away from it, or discard it as finished, condemned, or a "throw-away." God *loves* the world he created; so much that he gave his one and only son for it (John 3:16-17). God sent his only son Jesus into it, and in the same way, Jesus sends *you* into it. This is why he said in John 20:21, "As the Father has sent Me, I also send you."

Jesus has been given the nations to rule and heal the world, and *we* are the means by which that is to occur! If we really believe he is Lord over all, then make no mistake about it, he *will have* the world. And *we*, the expanding body of Christ, are the way that he will.

The gospel Jesus preached was not about saying a prayer and getting into heaven someday. It was so much more than that. It was a message of the Kingdom of God, transforming us, manifesting in and through us (as we enter a restored, intimate relationship with him), and expanding the dominion of Heaven culture on Earth.

Jesus said, "it is finished," and "behold I am making all things new." This is what we might call an "already but not yet" reality. You were made new through the finished work of the Cross ("Therefore, if anyone is in Christ, he is a new creation." 2 Corinthians 5:17). Yet, even though this is true, and stated in past tense, you are also still in *process* of manifesting this reality more and more, as his newness permeates more and more of your being. I propose that it is the same with the entire world and creation. The provision for a new Heaven and Earth is finished, yet we see the incremental process of "making all things new" manifested through Christ, in his people, spreading the culture of his kingdom throughout the world. So, whether in the micro (personal) sense, or macro (universal) sense, the principles of gradual kingdom expansion are the same.

The children of Israel were instructed to take the land *incrementally*. It is the same idea here. But we must not look back on our past bondage to sin (which Egypt represented in the story). Looking *forward*, we must rid our perceptions of fear of the "giants." I believe that in order to take the land (the world) by storm with the goodness of his kingdom, we must take on the giants. One of those giants we must conquer is an End Times belief that promotes fear, keeping us hindered and hiding out, waiting to be saved. Instead, we must realize that we have already been saved, and we are to go and spread this freedom to all of creation (Romans 8:21).

As my friend Johnny Ova (pastor of Sound of Heaven Church in Deer Park, NY) has so passionately stated, "a doctrine that takes the power and authority out of your hands is a doctrine of demons!" Jesus gained back all power and authority at the cross, and you are *in* him (as he is *in* you). So go, take over the world with the goodness and relentless sacrificial love found in his kingdom! (John 28:18-20)

Remember, you are his co-laborer and agent of change in the world around you, one person and one relationship at a time. May you build simply on a foundation of Christ in your life lived richly in him. This is his original intent for you. You are called for such a time as this. In Christ, you have been saved, healed, delivered, and raised up to be a part of his very bride — one with him. Together, we are his body, the Church, against whom the gates of hell cannot stand, and we are growing and expanding to fill all things. All creation is waiting for us to realize this, to manifest this, and to take our place as the sons of God!

NOTES

NOTES

_____

_____

_____

_____

_____

_____

_____

_____

_____

NOTES

NOTES

_____

_____

_____

_____

_____

_____

_____

_____

_____

_____

ABOUT THE AUTHOR

Evan Doukas is a lover of Jesus. As a messenger of the Gospel, his core passion is to see the restorative and transformative culture of God's Kingdom revealed in all creation—from the heart of man to the land itself. He believes the Gospel's cosmic rescue story carries deep and tangible impact for our lives and for the Earth, and he delights in helping others embrace their place within it. Evan is a devoted husband to his beloved wife, Kirsten, and a father to their two beautiful daughters.

SeraphCreative

Heaven's Heart for Earth

Seraph Creative is a collective of artists, writers, theologians & illustrators who desire to see the body of Christ grow into full maturity, walking in their inheritance as Sons of God on the Earth.

Sign up to our newsletter to know about future exciting releases.

Visit our website: www.seraphcreative.org

www.ingramcontent.com/pod-product-compliance
Lightning Source LLC
Chambersburg PA
CBHW051234120626
46547CB00013B/1639